curious?about

GREAT WHITE SHARKS

BY MONIKA DAVIES

AMICUS LEARNING

What are you

1 CHAPTER ONE
Meet the Great White Shark
PAGE 4

2 CHAPTER TWO
Great White Shark Behaviors
PAGE 10

curious about?

3
CHAPTER THREE

Life in the Ocean

PAGE
16

Stay Curious! Learn More . . .22
Glossary 24
Index 24

Curious About is published by
Amicus Learning, an imprint of Amicus
P.O. Box 227, Mankato, MN 56002
www.amicuspublishing.us

Editor: Ana Brauer
Series Designer: Kathleen Petelinsek
Book Designer and Photo Researcher: Sara Hood

Library of Congress Cataloging-in-Publication Data
Names: Davies, Monika, author.
Title: Curious about great white sharks / by Monika Davies.
Description: Mankato, MN : Amicus Learning, an imprint of Amicus, [2026] | Series: Curious about sharks | Includes bibliographical references and index. | Audience: Ages 6–9 | Audience: Grades 2–3 | Summary: "Where do great white sharks live? Are they endangered? Learn about this giant ocean apex predator in this question-and-answer book for elementary-aged readers. Includes infographics, table of contents, glossary, books and websites for further research, and index"— Provided by publisher.
Identifiers: LCCN 2024048306 (print) | LCCN 2024048307 (ebook) | ISBN 9798892005043 (library binding) | ISBN 9798892005586 (paperback) | ISBN 9798892006125 (ebook)
Subjects: LCSH: White shark—Juvenile literature.
Classification: LCC QL638.95.L3 D37 2026 (print) | LCC QL638.95.L3 (ebook) | DDC 597.3/3—dc23/eng/20241226
LC record available at https://lccn.loc.gov/2024048306
LC ebook record available at https://lccn.loc.gov/2024048307

Photo Credits: Alamy Stock Photo/Chris & Monique Fallows, 13, David Fleetham, 9, Frank Pey, cover, 1, Pascal Kobeh, 6–7, Reinhard Dirscherl, 10–11, WaterFrame_dpr, 2, 14–15; Getty Images/by wildestanimal, 2, 5, 18–19, Chris Clor, 16, Ken Kiefer 2, 3, 20–21, Taken by Andrew Thirlwell, 17; Shutterstock/BW Folsom, 8, xiaorui, 8; The Noun Project/Adrien Coquet, 22, Delwar Hossain, 22, IronSV, 23, Yosua Bungaran, 23; Vecteezy/om1947, 7

Printed in India

CHAPTER ONE

Why are they called great white sharks?

They are 'great' in size. Most female sharks grow up to 16 feet (4.9 meters) long. Males grow up to 13 feet (4 m) long. Their white bellies give them their name. Great white sharks are apex **predators**. They are at the top of the ocean food chain.

DID YOU KNOW?
Great white sharks are also called white sharks. But many people just call them great whites.

Great white sharks can live up to 70 years.

Can I swim with one?

Maybe, but it's not recommended. Great whites swim in every ocean. They like to stay in warm water close to land. This is where they find plenty to eat. Great whites do not usually eat humans. But it is safer to avoid these strong and curious hunters.

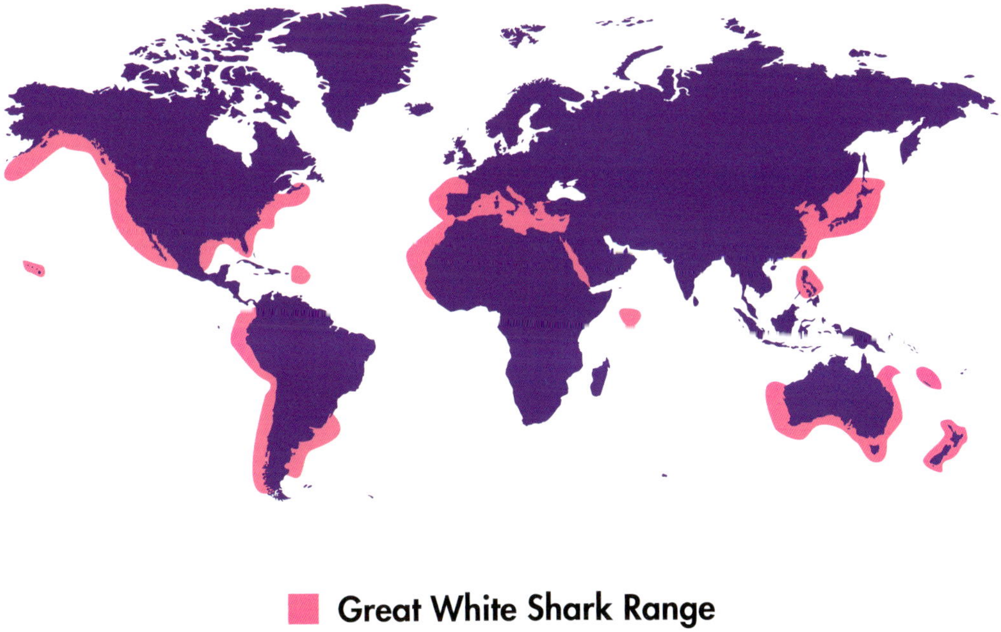

Some divers are trained to swim with sharks. They know how to stay safe.

How many teeth do great whites have?

More than 300! Great whites have a sharp, toothy grin. Their teeth are set in seven rows. Their teeth have a saw-like edge. Great whites use their teeth to break bones and cut up **prey**.

DID YOU KNOW?

Each tooth of a great white shark is 2.5 inches (6.4 centimeters) long. This is about the same size as the top of a pop can.

Sharks grow new teeth throughout their lives. When a tooth falls out, a new one will grow.

CHAPTER TWO

How do great whites hunt?

Great whites have the best sense of smell of any shark.

Great whites use their sharp senses to hunt. They can spot prey in the dark. Their ears can pick up tiny motions nearby. Great whites also have a great sense of smell. They can smell a drop of blood from about 0.25 miles (0.40 kilometers) away!

What do great whites eat?

Great whites are not picky eaters! Baby sharks often eat fish, squid, and smaller sharks. Adult sharks dine on bigger **mammals**. Their menu usually includes seals and sea lions. Sometimes the sharks jump out of the water to catch their dinner.

When a shark jumps out of the water, it is called breaching.

Are great whites cold-blooded?

Most sharks are **cold-blooded**. Their body temperature matches the water they swim in. But great whites are **warm-blooded**! They can make their body warmer than the ocean. This gives them extra **energy** for hunting.

Great whites can hunt in cold or warm water because they are warm-blooded.

How do great white shark babies grow up?

On their own! Great whites might have a litter of up to 10 pups. But these baby sharks do not stay with their mom after birth. In fact, they swim away from her in case she eats them!

DID YOU KNOW?
A baby great white shark is around 5 feet (1.5 m) long. That's the size of a standard bathtub!

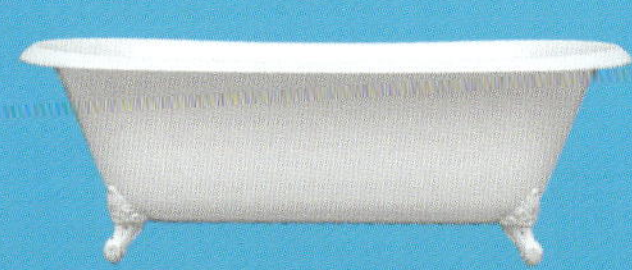

Sharks are considered adults after 10 to 16 years.

Do great whites sleep?

Scientists think sharks only sleep for 10 minutes at a time.

Not like we do. They just keep swimming! Great white sharks get oxygen through their **gills** as they move through water. The sharks do not close their eyes to sleep. But they do seem to sleep. To rest, they open their jaw. They then slowly drift.

GLOSSARY

cold-blooded Having a body temperature that changes with the temperature of the air or water.

energy The ability to move or be active.

gill A body part that a fish uses to breathe underwater.

mammal A kind of animal that feeds milk to its babies and often has hair or fur covering its skin.

predator An animal that eats other animals for food.

prey An animal that is hunted by another animal for food.

vulnerable A species considered to be facing a high risk of extinction in the wild.

warm-blooded Having a body temperature that remains steady and warm, no matter what the outside temperature is.

INDEX

babies, 12, 16
food, 4, 12
Jaws, 21
ranges, 7
senses, 11
size, 4, 8, 16
sleep, 18–19
teeth, 8–9, 21
warm-blooded, 14, 15

About the Author

Monika Davies is a Canadian author of over 60 books for young readers. She thinks sharks are fascinating—and hopes you agree! When Monika isn't writing, you can find her strolling by the ocean, reading books too quickly, or trying to keep her seven plants alive.